SOME THOUGHTS ON UNIVERSITY EDUCATION

T0346163

NATIONAL BOOK LEAGUE FIFTH ANNUAL LECTURE

SOME THOUGHTS ON UNIVERSITY EDUCATION

SIR RICHARD LIVINGSTONE

LONDON

PUBLISHED FOR THE

NATIONAL BOOK LEAGUE

BY THE CAMBRIDGE UNIVERSITY PRESS

1948

CAMBRIDGE
UNIVERSITY PRESS

University Printing House, Cambridge CB2 8BS, United Kingdom

Cambridge University Press is part of the University of Cambridge.

It furthers the University's mission by disseminating knowledge in the pursuit of education, learning and research at the highest international levels of excellence.

www.cambridge.org
Information on this title: www.cambridge.org/9781316620090

© Cambridge University Press 1948

First published 1948
First paperback edition 2016

A catalogue record for this publication is available from the British Library

ISBN 978-1-316-62009-0 Paperback

SOME THOUGHTS ON
UNIVERSITY EDUCATION

THIS lecture consists mainly of criticism: so, to correct the impression which it might otherwise leave, let me begin by saying that in my opinion the last forty years have been a time of steady improvement in the universities. It is not only that they have grown in size and resources, that they are infinitely better fitted in equipment and organization for their work, that there is teaching and research in far more subjects, that the number of students has greatly increased and is drawn from all classes in the nation, but that they are alive with that vitality with which this age at its best challenges its difficulties and responds to its opportunities. This rosy picture may be due to the complacency of advancing years, and members of the younger generation, who are the natural critics of the present and the makers of the future, may complain that the tints are too bright. I can only state my own impression. At the same time I believe that, as places of undergraduate education (and this, no less than research, is the university's duty), they need reform, and that the future will be astonished that we have done nothing to remedy grave weaknesses in our system. Naturally I am speaking within the limits of my own experience: my criticisms may not be true of every British university: but I believe that the general principles which this lecture urges are sound.

If you wished to destroy modern civilization, the most effective way to do it would be to abolish universities. They stand at its centre. They create knowledge and train minds. The education which they give moulds the outlook of all educated men, and thus affects politics, administration, the professions, industry and commerce. Their discoveries and their thought penetrate almost every activity of life. The technique of the doctor and the miner, the pronouncements of the pulpit, and even of the Press, the measures of Governments are dictated or at least modified by these distant nerve-centres of intelligence, and on their health and vigour the well-being of the whole modern world depends. They add nothing to the amount of natural intelligence existing, but they refine and perfect what exists and fit it to serve purposes and take stresses which in its raw form it could not meet. Their influence is increasing and will increase unless there is a collapse of modern civilization. They have an influence on our world which is almost as great as that of the Church on the Middle Ages, and in many ways it is a similar influence.

Now let the *advocatus diaboli* speak: "Do you not notice", he will say to us, "a serious limitation to the influence of the university on our civilization? Our gravest problem is moral, spiritual. But what effect has the university on the spiritual and moral life of the world, or even on its political life so far as this is determined by spiritual and moral forces? It was not always so. Witness the originating and controlling influence of the University of Paris in the thirteenth and early fourteenth centuries; of Oxford and Cambridge in preparing the Reformation in this country in a later day, of Fichte and others in early nineteenth-century Germany. In the last twenty years two new conceptions of life have changed the course of the world—Communism and Nazism. The universities have not created or moulded them; like mercenaries, they have served the rulers of the day in Russia, Germany, Italy; supplied them with the weapons they need and asked no questions. Outside the countries which accepted these philosophies, the universities have provided no alternate philosophy to counteract them. We have the spectacle of the democratic countries, conscious of deep detestation of philosophies of race and power, clinging to the traditions and memories of a nobler view of life and to values which they dimly discern but cannot formulate into a clear rational ideal. The universities do not help them. If it is too much to expect the universities to formulate an ideal, they might at least have sent out men who would have done it, given the guidance for which the world is looking, and led it not only in economics and sociology, in physics and chemistry, but in even more important things. They have not done so.

> Achilles ponders in his tent;
> _ The kings of modern thought are dumb;
> Silent they sit and not content,
>   And wait to see the future come.

They do not regard spiritual ideals, except the ideal of knowledge, as their business; ultimate ends are not their concern; they provide the tools of civilization but give no guidance for their use. The war could not have been waged, or at least would have been very different without them. But they did nothing to prevent or end it, or limit its savagery and destructiveness. Science served both sides with complete impartiality and provided alike penicillin and radar, the V2 and the atomic bomb." I compared the rôle of the university today to that of the Church in the Middle Ages. A very important difference between the two is apparent.

Hence a certain restiveness about the position of the university. On the one hand it is denounced as a liberal-bourgeois institution—the familiar clichés betray the source of this attack—from an opposite angle Christian critics deplore that it fails to give any interpretation of life or guide to conduct, and is indifferent to any values except truth,

Holding no form of creed,
But contemplating all.

To such critics the reply of the university is that the god worshipped in its shrine is neither utility nor success nor social progress, nor even goodness, but truth; that its concern is knowledge, the vision of reality, that the condition of its existence is complete freedom to see things as they are; that its ideal is the ideal of Socrates "to follow the argument where it leads", and its prayer the prayer of the dying Goethe, "More light"; or even that of Ajax in the mist, ἐν δὲ φάει καὶ ὄλεσσον "Light, though I perish in the light". If critics say that this unchartered freedom, this indifference to anything but knowledge may lead to disaster either through the destruction of beliefs necessary to society or through discoveries like the atomic bomb or chemical warfare, the answer is that history is full of warnings against the sacrifice of truth to edification, that the pursuit of knowledge has led mankind, by however dangerous paths, steadily upward, and that to think or act otherwise is to fail in faith. Here is the answer to those who complain that the university is amoral, indifferent to values, concerned with nothing except knowledge.

And is not the pursuit of knowledge in itself the child and the parent of moral qualities? Does it not require, for any measure of success, industry, perseverance, disinterestedness, faith, and above all truth? Are these not virtues and values? If one was inquiring into the moral influence of the university, it is in these directions that we should find it, and in the general civilizing influence which its studies exert.

Ingenuas didicisse fideliter artes
Emollit mores nec sinit esse feros.

Of all human virtues perhaps truth is the rarest and most difficult: blindness of mind, prepossessions and the protean forms of egoism continually assail it. Necessarily it is the *genius loci* of an institution devoted to advancing knowledge. The result of studying in a university is that the student at least comes in contact with it. The condition of teaching in a university is that a man should profess it as his aim, and if his devotion grows dull the critical atmosphere which surrounds him is a whetstone to sharpen its edge. As Aristotle said, we acquire virtues by practising them, and in universities truth is perforce practised. The university is the chief generating station of it, the power-house from which it is diffused through the community. Is not that much? it will be asked. Is it indeed not enough? And if more is asked of the university, may it not be deflected from its true purpose and may not its great and proper virtue be impaired? So the university might reply.

And yet we may feel that this is not a complete answer to the charge. We may recognize the great services of the university to society, but wish them to be greater still. The condition of the world requires it. The position of the universities in modern civilization gives them a unique opportunity and a compelling responsibility. In 1852 Newman thus defined the function of the university. "If a practical end must be assigned to a university course, then I say it is training good members of society."[1] Unless we take the words "good members of society" in a narrow sense, not only the achievement but the aim of the modern university falls short of this. Yet Newman was writing at a time when the condition of the world was far more stable and the minds of men far less confused than they are today. How much stronger the case is for his view in an age when with divided and uncertain

[1] *The Scope and Nature of University Education*; Discourse 6.

11

minds we have to ride the storms of social and intellectual change! The university should equip us for this task too. It should train men to be not merely masters of a special field but to know what Plato meant when he wished his ruling class to learn to be "spectators of all time and all existence". It should have wide aims and a sense of practical needs: and its graduates should go into life not so much expert in the battle-cries and tactics of the moment, as conscious of the deeper issues at stake and of the values involved in them. The churches and the universities are the natural institutions to see to this; and unfortunately the churches have lost their hold on many whom the university reaches. If it does not undertake the task, in the end we may find, as in Russia and in Hitler's Germany, that the State will dictate a philosophy of life to the nation; or we shall drift with no philosophy at all. Either alternative is dismal.

Why does the university fail to achieve what Newman wished? My answer would be that, while there has been some thought about the organization and administration of universities, there has been very little about the education which they give to undergraduates; and this is their weakest side. In detail it is often excellent; the individual courses, though no doubt capable of improvement, are in general well designed and taught. But undergraduate education has never been thought out as a whole. It has simply grown, and its development has been determined by a combination of *vis inertiae*, the pressure of circumstances and a struggle of individual subjects for a place in the sun. We are all familiar with the process by which the curriculum develops. A subject, long neglected, makes its way into the circle, establishes a position, and then pushes out from its base to seize as much of the country as finance and its rivals and public opinion allow.

In fact university education has grown up in the casual English way. It has never been viewed, much less planned, as a whole. A cynic might give a book on the subject the title of "Drift".

Let us glance at some of the circumstances which have moulded and are moulding the development of undergraduate education. The first is a sense of the importance of thoroughness, a dislike of superficiality, of merely dipping the feet into the waters of knowledge and not plunging into their depths. This instinct is sound and this influence good.

The second influence is the immense growth of knowledge. Aristotle could write great works on a dozen subjects. Today the field of one physicist may be almost a foreign country to another, and his time is fully occupied if he is to be a master in his own. Things are no better in other fields. Thirty years ago a college tutor in Oxford was prepared to teach for the whole modern history curriculum. Today he is a mediaevalist or a modernist, and even so has to specialize in a branch of his subject. Specialism is a condition of knowledge. This influence pushes us in the same direction as the former and we have to recognize and make terms with it. It will increase.

So far I have spoken of forces which, if dangerous, are inevitable and in themselves good. But there are other influences which are powerful but unnecessary and bad. There are the highly specialized scholarship examinations at the older universities which cause the pupil who has passed the School Certificate examination at the age of fifteen to concentrate henceforward, often on a single field of study, and usually on the one which he will study in the university, neglecting other subjects indispensable to a full education. Finally, financial motives contribute to narrow education at the university. There are a number of students for whom a pass curriculum is educationally

13

better than the specialized honours course. But, especially in teaching, an honours degree is more marketable in the outside world than a pass degree. So financial considerations override education, and the third and fourth classes in the Honour School lists reveal the ill-advised efforts of many who have struggled with a course beyond their abilities. The same evil, due to a different cause, can be seen at Oxford and Cambridge in the case of women students who, having been driven to specialize at school by the high standard of admission, are then driven by their colleges' requirements of an honours degree to specialize still further at the university, probably in the same subject as they studied at school.

Under the continuous pressure of such forces as I have mentioned, growth is haphazard: the parts may flourish but a sense of the whole is lost. Horace speaks of writers whose poems abound in brilliant purple patches but fail in total effect. The criticism might be applied to most of our own undergraduate education. Its weakness is an exclusive specialism which there is no attempt to counteract. The specialism, roughly speaking, is in either science or mathematics or the humanities. Science concentrates on nature and ignores man: the humanities concentrate on man and ignore nature. All "specialism enhances the centrifugal forces in society",[1] but scientific and mathematical specialism is, for the aims with which I am dealing, the most dangerous. It is not directly concerned with the human problem (though it has a great influence on it). The scientist, it has been said, explains everything but himself. Nor is it concerned with human values. The words good and evil do not naturally come into its vocabulary. Further, to deal exclusively with atoms, elements and cells is a bad preparation for dealing with or understanding human beings or human problems;

[1] *Harvard Report*, p. 53.

indeed it is no preparation at all. This is the more serious because the influence of science and the need for scientists will increase. It is significant that the numbers offering science as their main subject in the Higher Certificate increased from 44 per cent in 1939 to 53 per cent in 1946; it is melancholy to reflect how narrow the education of most of that 53 per cent was. The balance may well continue to swing in the direction of science. It is idle to attempt to counterbalance the swing by a greater output of graduates in the humanities, unless the country needs them and they can find employment. The true remedy is to see that the education of scientists includes such training in the humanities, as will enable them to play their full part in national life, not merely as superior technicians or expert specialists, but as citizens and directors of policy.

Now turn to the humanities. Specialism here has its own obvious weaknesses with which I am not now concerned, but at any rate these studies are in the human field, and they should give what is needed to train Newman's "good members of society". Literature reflects all the thoughts and feelings of man; religion and philosophy deal with his attempts to understand his nature, his place in the universe, and the principles that should regulate his conduct; history records his adventures in society. All these keep or should keep the human problem continually before the mind and show ways of interpreting it. This indeed is not true of all the humanities: economics, for instance, cover only a narrow segment of life and that (as usually taught) in a narrow way, and is of little more use for our purpose than chemistry or physics. The best studies are those in which, as in the classical school at Oxford (I take my instances from the university which I know best), history, philosophy and literature are combined; or where, as in Modern Greats, economics are combined with philosophy. I once asked an eminent banker

15

what subjects a man who wished to go into business should study at the university: his answer was "Economics, and, of course, philosophy". The significant words here are "of course".

But it is a question not merely of the subjects to be studied but of the way in which we study them. Salt can lose its savour; the humanities can lose their humanity. Education continually tends to degenerate into technique, and the life tends to go out of all subjects when they become technical. It is possible to read Plato's *Republic*, as I did when an undergraduate, without realizing that it deals with the deepest of all problems—what the good life is, why men should wish to live it, how a state can be created in which it can be lived. It is possible to read the *Oedipus Tyrannus* of Sophocles without realizing that its characters are people as alive as ourselves, reacting as we might to the impact of tragic events. Professor Whitehead remarks of his own schooldays: "We studied some plays of Shakespeare which were the worst feature of all. To this day I cannot read *King Lear*, having had the advantage of studying it accurately at school."[1] It is possible to read history and get a history scholarship and an honours degree in it without divining the deeps that lie beneath laws and wars, diplomacy and institutions, or hearing behind the tumult and the shouting the still sad music of humanity: indeed that music is inaudible in most history books, though always present in the great ones. So easily can education decline into routine and mechanism.

That is one of the dangers which we have to face. Another, allied to it, much more respectable, and perhaps less easily escaped, is inherent in the nature of modern scholarship. Exact knowledge is a condition of all study, and to acquire it the scholar must learn the techniques by which knowledge is won. A historian for instance must

[1] *Essays in Science and Philosophy*, p. 37.

16

know the necessary languages and have a training in diplomacy and palaeography and the examination of sources and authorities—each of them a study in itself. As soon as he is equipped for his work, he finds himself in the vast continent of history, a continent with many countries, themselves divided into many provinces, which in turn have many districts—politics, diplomacy, war by sea or land, law, constitutional history, religion, art, science, archaeology, geography, social conditions, the life of the common people, the lives of great men. He throws himself into the minute and exhausting task of mastering some unexplored corner of this continent, and to this end must study every detail of his field and know anything that can throw light on it—including the work of other scholars of his own and of foreign countries. Such is modern research. If you wish to see the burden which the modern scholar has to bear, look at the admirable edition of Rashdall's great work on the universities by Powicke and Emden; the footnotes reveal how much detailed knowledge was required merely to bring up to date a book which itself was a work of elaborate and exact research.

Now three things may happen. Under the hands of a scholar like Maitland or Acton or Fisher (I only mention the dead), the parable of Ezekiel will be enacted. The historian will cause breath to enter into the dry bones and they will come together, bone to his bone; and lo, the sinews and the flesh will come upon them and the skin cover them and they will live.[1] We shall have real men, living issues, great history, an instrument of true education.

But the result may be less fortunate. The mass of the material may crush the student and the dust stifle him; at least it may dull his freshness and deaden his imagination. The facts which he has laboriously collected may serve the purposes of others, but he will not bring them to life.

[1] Ezekiel, xxxvii.

To do that is an even harder task than the labours of research. "When once Dryasdust has done his work within us . . . , we use our free formative imagination. . . . The tradition is dead: our task is to revivify life that has passed away. We know that ghosts cannot speak until they have drunk blood; and the spirits which we evoke demand the blood of our hearts."[1]

Or again, another danger. Knowledge may become an end in itself, irrespective of whether it is worth knowing. The scholar is seduced by his technique. So we see Housman, a man of penetrating and poetic imagination, giving years of his life to studying a third-rate writer like Manilius. It is of such research that Jowett said "That sort of learning is a great power if a man can only keep his mind above it". It may have its justification;

> High heaven neglects the lore
> Of nicely calculated less and more;

and worldliness is a disease in scholarship as elsewhere. But the scholar who takes this line at least risks losing a sense of proportion and forgetting that outside his narrow world is a greater world of which it is only a part. This is not what is meant by the humanities in the full and true sense of the word.

I am not of course denying that minute research is essential or suggesting that specialism is bad; both are necessary, and, apart from that, specialism is educationally sound; without it the student will neither get knowledge nor know what it is. I am only arguing that we should be aware of a tendency in the humanities to develop their less humane aspects, and in *all* subjects to become ends in themselves and to lose contact with life, and in so far to contribute little or nothing to humanizing their students.

[1] Wilamowitz-Moellendorf, *On Greek Historical Writing* (Clarendon Press), p. 25.

Hitherto I have argued that, though our universities play an immense part in modern civilization, it is not a directing part, that mainly they serve aims set by others; and that this implies some defect in the education which they give. I have suggested that this defect lies in their undergraduate studies; that these have been shaped by the pressure of circumstances and not by clear thought directed to definite ends; that the exaggerated specialism in science which ignores human problems is obviously bad and absurd, but that the study of the humanities often has its weaknesses too; and that our system needs re-thinking and remodelling so that it may give the student an outlook and attitude which will enable him to live effectively in the world.

Let me now glance at an attempt to do this, which is being made in America. There has been some thought about the undergraduate curriculum in Britain, especially in the civic universities. But in America there has been more thought, clearer thought, and, what is equally important, definite action. That is partly due to differences in the educational system of the two countries, and in particular to the inferiority of American secondary education to our own. The school in America sends out its pupils less advanced and less well-prepared for university work than here, and the university has therefore to undertake some of the tasks which in theory are here performed by the school. Hence, the peculiar character of the American college, to which we have no exact parallel. But, apart from this necessity, the Americans have realized that general education cannot be completed at school, that literature and history and the social sciences are studied with far more understanding by the undergraduate than by the schoolboy; not to mention philosophy, which is beyond the ordinary schoolboy's grasp. This explains American concern with the problem of general education at the university. Of special interest are recent developments in this field at Harvard, Yale, Columbia, Chicago, Michigan and elsewhere. In the plan expounded in the interesting Harvard report on *General Education in a Free Society*, it is proposed that all undergraduates at Harvard College should take a full course in the Humanities, in the Social Sciences and in either the Physical or Biological Sciences, in order that every student should be introduced to the major problems and determining forces of modern civilization. If the resulting curriculum successfully combines these courses with adequate specialization in some major subject, the American undergraduate will be better educated for life than many of our own.

I know the danger of arguing from American universities to our own. Comparisons are as fallacious as they are easy, and I am not suggesting that these American experiments can be engrafted on our system. But it is legitimate to point out how clearly the Americans have seen a problem which is also ours. The framers of these plans have asked themselves what is the minimum equipment needed by an educated man if he is to live intelligently in the modern world. They have answered that he must be aware of the chief social and political problems; that he must have an idea of the nature and power of science; and that he should learn something of the spiritual forces which alone give meaning and value to human existence, in order that, in Milton's words, he may become fit "to perform justly, skilfully and magnanimously all the offices, both private and public of peace and war". All the adverbs in this quotation are important; the one most easily overlooked is the last.

This is a broader and deeper conception of the problem than is common with us. We are apt to speak as if the need was to provide a more all-round education, to see that the humanists know something about science and that the scientists know something about literature and history; this of course is essential, if education is to produce educated men. But to end there is to halt halfway. The most important task of education is to bring home to the student the greatest of all problems—the problem of living—and to give him some guidance in it. Nations and individuals are ultimately judged by the values and standards by which they are ruled. "The noblest of all studies", said Plato, "is the study of what a man should be and how he should live." Some room for this study should be found in every education and every university, for though our science or sociology or political and economic planning may be defective, their weaknesses are neither so great nor so serious as our spiritual and moral defects.

"Whatever the world thinks," said Bishop Berkeley, "he who hath not much meditated upon God, the human mind and the Summum Bonum, may possibly make a thriving earthworm, but will certainly make a sorry patriot and a sorry statesman." Burke said much the same thing in different words: "We should auspicate all our proceedings with the old warning of the Church, Sursum corda." Certainly some difference can be noted between statesmen like Masaryk and Smuts, and in earlier days, Burke and Gladstone, who so "auspicated their proceedings" and who "meditated much upon God and the Summum Bonum and the human mind", and those who have not. The former belong to all time as well as to their own age, for they have seen its issues in a permanent setting as well as in their immediate context. Such meditation gives the mind a peculiar quality. It reminds us that in Aristotle's words, "there are other things far more divine than man"[1]; it liberates the mind

[1] *E.N.* 1141 b 1.

from the provincialism which is unaware of forces and issues beyond its immediate view and customary range; it gives the sense of perspective, which distinguishes the accident from the substance, the ephemeral from the permanent; it helps us to see the present in the light of all time and all existence. But the ordinary man as well as the politician—and in days of universal suffrage everyone is a politician—needs a sense of perspective, an awareness of "things far more divine than man". They are a part of knowledge—of a knowledge so important that to ignore it is to accept a purblind view of life.

And there is an even more important side to this "meditation on God, the human mind and the Summum Bonum". It is a road to something that everyone needs, a philosophy of life. "In the beginning everything was in confusion; then Mind came and ordered the chaos." So Anaxagoras summarises the creation of the Cosmos or ordered universe. A less ambitious but necessary task is imposed on every human being—to set their own lives in order—and the chief instrument for the purpose is the reason. We are born into the foreign country of the world: we have to live in it and find our way about it. There is no choice in the matter. We shall drift on the currents of chance desires, of the mood of the day, of the pressure of circumstances, unless we can appeal to some definite principle:

> A light to guide,
> To check the erring and reprove;
> Thou who art victory and law
> When empty terrors overawe;
> From vain temptations dost set free;
> And calm'st the weary strife of frail humanity.

It is idle to murmur agnosticism. Of course everyone is agnostic in the sense that they are ready to change their minds if convinced that their opinions are wrong. But this does not mean that we are to have no opinions on subjects because they are difficult and obscure. We have to act: every action implies some view of life: so though the meaning of life and the problem of conduct are subjects no less debated and uncertain than the problem of religion, immediately we act we express a view about them. How necessary then that we should have a philosophy of living, for shaping conduct, for reference in doubt, for challenge, stimulus, and driving power! How strange if at a time when all agree that we must understand or at least have a theory of nature so that we may control it, the importance of a rational theory on which to base conduct is not equally apparent! How paradoxical if an age of rationalism should not feel the need of a reasoned philosophy of life! Higher education would not have done its work if it sent out the student unable to write English or wholly ignorant of English history and literature, or unaware of the importance and nature of science. But is it not even more disastrous if it leaves him without a philosophy of life, however provisional, a definite view of the ends to which it should be directed and of the principles by which it should be ruled, a clear idea of good and bad in conduct?

Yet what do our universities do to help their pupils towards such a philosophy? There is little in the universities to encourage the meditations which Berkeley thought an essential part of education. The direct road to them is through religion or philosophy: under the guidance of some teachers literature and history may be by-paths of approach. But under our present system there is no guarantee that all students will travel any of those roads, and the great majority never set foot on them. In Oxford and Cambridge, Christianity is represented by College Chapels and Chaplains, and theology is included in degree courses there and elsewhere. Philosophy can be studied

23

in any university, but finds few followers in most, except at Oxford, where it is an integral part of the important schools of "Greats" and "Modern Greats". Only in Scotland, where it is a compulsory subject for the ordinary M.A. (but not for Honours Degrees, where it is equally desirable), is philosophy recognized as a study without which education is incomplete. Here, Scotland leads England; but unfortunately England does not follow. Religion is squeezed out of many secondary schools by the preparation for scholarships; religion and philosophy are for most students squeezed out of the university by preparation for a specialized degree.

The Americans have seen the need and proposed to meet it by the compulsory course in the humanities, to be taken by every student during his first two years at college and called in the Harvard Report the study of the "Great Texts of Literature". Its aim is "familiarity with as much of the greatest writings as can be read and pondered in the limited time available. A list from which a selection would be made might include Homer, one or two of the Greek tragedies, Plato, the Bible, Virgil, Dante, Shakespeare, Milton, Tolstoy."[1] The Harvard proposals ignore religion on grounds which seem prudential rather than educational, and, for other reasons, leave philosophy as an optional subject,[2] though they make an interesting suggestion about it. "Western culture may be compared to a lake fed by the streams of Hellenism, Christianity, science, and democracy. A philosophical course based upon the study of these contributions might offer an extremely valuable way of considering the conceptions of a life of reason, the principle of an ordered and intelligible world, the ideas of faith, of a personal God, of the absolute value of the human individual, the method of observation and experi-

[1] *General Education in a Free Society*, p. 206 f.   [2] *Ibid.*, p. 209 f.

24

ment, and the conception of empirical laws, as well as the doctrines of equality and of the brotherhood of man."[1] For those who do not take philosophy, its place is to be taken by the study of the "Great Texts of Literature", and this is not conceived as a mere literary study, but as something much more important. "The humanities point both to moral and to aesthetic values." They give "direct access to the potentialities and norms of living as they are presented by the best authors. *All work in literature should be concerned chiefly with making these visions accessible.*"[2] In fact the aim of the Harvard reforms is to satisfy in one way or another the demand which Berkeley made.

Undoubtedly history and literature, studied deliberately with this aim in view—and the qualification is important —do reveal the powers, values and development of the human spirit. But it would be better to approach the problem more directly and to make a study of religion or of philosophy an essential element in every university course. Whatever we may think about it, religion is the most important of all subjects, both in history and in itself, and to ignore it is to narrow the outlook and starve the mind. By religion I mean a study of what we should think of the meaning and ultimate nature of the universe; how, in the light of the view we form, we should live: the different answers which have been given to these questions by great religious thinkers[3]. Philosophy treats the general problems of religion from a more detached and general point of view.

I know the objections which the wary academic mind

[1] *General Education in a Free Society*, p. 211.

[2] *Ibid.*, pp. 73, 107 (the italics are mine).

[3] Cf. Tolstoi's definition (*Life*, II, 426): "True religion is a relation, accordant with reason and knowledge, which man establishes with the infinite life surrounding him, and which is such as binds his life to that infinity and guides his conduct."

raises in the face of new proposals, and no doubt will bring against the insertion of philosophy and/or religion in a university course. "There is no time for it." Time can always be found for what is essential. "Many students will get nothing out of it." Some students will not: others will; but all need it. If subjects are dropped because some students do not profit by them, our curricula would consist of gaps. "It is unfair to ask philosophers to lecture on an elementary level." They do so in Scottish universities. Nobody is the worse for having to express himself so that ordinary people can understand him. Plato and Socrates did not find it impossible to be intelligible to others besides philosophic experts. "What is the use of the average student studying logic or metaphysics?" They will do him no harm—especially logic. But of course for our purpose ethics are the important subject: and whatever philosophy is chosen it must be studied for the light it can throw on the business of living.

So far as books are concerned, I think that much the best and most stimulating single introduction to these problems is Plato's *Republic*, now accessible in Professor Cornford's brilliant translation with notes for English readers.[1] It has special advantages for the purpose. "The Greeks", said Nietzsche, "are simple, like genius; therefore they are the immortal teachers"; and certainly Plato, in spite of the depths he sounds, is in a sense simple. Further, unlike so much philosophy, the *Republic* has the urgency and earnestness of a book springing from practical need. Plato had been a politician himself; he had seen the fall of the Athenian Empire and the corruption of a great democratic ideal; and he turned from politics to philosophy because the state of the contemporary world made him feel that the

[1] There are of course other good translations; but none of them have notes to give the guidance which a reader of Plato needs.

whole question of government needed thinking out afresh. Finally it raises so many problems. We call Plato's book the *Republic*: Plato called it "On goodness": it starts from the questions of two young Athenians who would like to believe in goodness, but find it difficult; and never has the difficulty been put more trenchantly than they put it. So, in the pages that follow, one after another the great problems rise: what is goodness; why should men believe in it; in what kind of state can the good life be best lived; what part in the state should be played by education; what is the right kind of education; what different ideals rule individuals and states, and to what kind of lives do they lead? We may not agree with Plato's answers to these problems, but when we have read him we shall have seen them through the eyes of one of the greatest of writers and men. The essential thing is that everyone should see them, whether by reading the *Republic* or in some better way. For they are the most important problems both for the individual and the world; and to be unaware of them or to have no rational view of them is to be uneducated. If the university ignores them, it will not train "good members of society".

To sum up. I began by suggesting that the influence of universities on the world is disappointingly limited; that this is due to their being too little concerned with ends, with human values, with a philosophy of life. Yet the world at any time is good or bad according to the values which rule it and which it embodies. Man "lives not in a world of hard facts to which 'thoughts' make no difference, but in a world of thoughts; if you change the moral, political and economic 'theories' generally accepted by the society in which he lives, you change the character of his world".[1] And the most important of these, the ones which most radically change the world, are moral theories.

[1] Collingwood, *Autobiography*, p. 147.

I suggest, therefore, that our undergraduate courses should be reconsidered, not with a view to altering their main lines, which are excellent, but to remedy this defect, and that some study of religion or philosophy or of both should be included in all. To claim this is no treason to the twin ideals of truth and knowledge. There is no question of indoctrination, of imposing beliefs. Opinion remains free. It is only the claim that no one should pass through the highest stages of education without considering the greatest problems of all, and taking at any rate some steps towards acquiring the most important of all knowledge. Then the universities may add to the influence which they now exert on the world an influence even more important, and send out into it men equipped, not merely to use and improve the means of life, but to direct and inspire its ends and to be instruments in its regeneration.

www.ingramcontent.com/pod-product-compliance
Ingram Content Group UK Ltd.
Pitfield, Milton Keynes, MK11 3LW, UK
UKHW042142280225
455719UK00001B/31

9 781316 620090